JOKE BOOK

EGMONT
We bring stories to life

First published in Great Britain 2014 by Egmont UK Limited
The Yellow Building, 1 Nicholas Road, London W11 4AN

ANGRY BIRDS ™ & © 2009 – 2014 Rovio Entertainment Ltd.
© 2014 Lucasfilm Ltd. & ® or ™ where indicated.
All rights reserved.

ISBN 978 1 4052 7359 6
58134/1
Printed in Great Britain

MEET THE TEAM!

BIRD REBELS

RED SKYWALKER

PRINCESS STELLA ORGANA

CHUCK 'HAM' SOLO

R2-EGG2

OBI-WAN KABOOMI

C-3P...

TEREBACCA

YODA BIRD

THE PORK FEDERATION

LARD VADER

EMPEROR PIGLATINE

PIGTROOPERS

BOBA FATT

GRAND MOFF TARKIN

HOG GUARD

JABBA THE HOG

BOWL THEM OVER, YODA!

WHY DOESN'T YODA BIRD LIKE RUGBY?

Because 'There is no try!'

WHY DID YODA BIRD CROSS THE ROAD?

Because the chickens "Forced" him to.

WHAT DO YOU GET IF YOU CROSS YODA BIRD, A FREEZER AND A POT OF PAINT?

Frozen Yodart!

TEREBACCA TWEETS!

WHAT DID HAM SOLO SAY WHEN HE DISCOVERED TEREBACCA WAS MISSING?

Hair today, gone tomorrow!

WHAT DO YOU GET WHEN TEREBACCA SITS IN YOUR VEGETABLE PATCH?

Squash!

WHICH SIDE OF TEREBACCA HAS THE MOST HAIR?

The outside!

WHAT HAPPENED WHEN TEREBACCA BROKE UP WITH HIS STARSHIP?

It became his ex-wing!

WHAT DO YOU CALL TEREBACCA WITH HIS HEAD UNDERWATER?

Anything you like!

WHO GRANTED TEREBACCA A WISH?

His hairy godmother!

WHAT DOES TEREBACCA PUT ON HIS CHRISTMAS TREE?

Hairy lights!

HOW DO PEOPLE FEEL WHEN THEY FIRST SEE TEREBACCA?

Tere-fied!

WHAT'S THE WORST PRESENT TO GET TEREBACCA FOR HIS BIRTHDAY?

A fur coat.

OBI-WAN KABOOMI SIZZLERS

WHAT DID OBI-WAN KABOOMI SAY TO RED WHEN THEY WERE PLAYING SNOOKER?
May the Force be with cue!

WHY DID OBI-WAN HAVE SUCH A TEMPER?
He kept blowing his top!

WHICH *STAR WARS* CHARACTER IS THE TASTIEST?
Obi-Wan Macaroni.

WHY IS OBI-WAN KABOOMI SO POPULAR?

He's got an explosive personality!

WHAT HAPPENED WHEN OBI-WAN KABOOMI WORKED AT A TRAIN STATION?

He became the station master!

WHAT DID THE DENTIST SAY TO OBI-WAN?

May the floss be with you!

WHAT TIME IS IT WHEN OBI-WAN KABOOMI GETS ANGRY?

Time to run for it!

WHAT DO YOU CALL SOMEONE WHO REALLY WANTS TO BE A JEDI?

Obi-Wannabe.

HOW DO THE BIRD ALLIANCE KEEP SO HEALTHY?

They have the best medical tweetment in the galaxy!

WHY WAS THE OWL THROWN OUT OF THE BIRD ALLIANCE?

Because he didn't give a hoot!

WHY WON'T THE BIRD ALLIANCE LET DUCKS JOIN?

Because they're all quackers!

WHY DID THE PARROT FLEE FROM THE BIRD ALLIANCE?

He was a polygon!

WHY DID LARD VADER LEAVE THE BIRD ALLIANCE?

He wanted to join the Pork Side!

WHY DO THE PIGTROOPERS WANT TO CAPTURE PRINCESS STELLA?

They like the look of the buns on her head!

WHERE DOESN'T PRINCESS STELLA ORGANA LIKE TO GO SHOPPING?

At the Darth Mall!

WHAT DO YOU CALL THE PRINCESS AT A FARMERS' MARKET?

Stella Organic!

WHY DOES PRINCESS STELLA KEEP HER HAIR TIED UP IN BUNS?

So it doesn't hang so-low!

WHY DID STELLA STICK HER HEAD OUT OF THE WINDOW?

She wanted to have bun in the sun!

WHY DID STELLA FEEL SORRY FOR THE REBEL PILOTS?

Because they were blue birds!

WHY DID OBI-WAN TAKE A SICK DAY?

He was feeling a little Force.

WHAT DID OBI-WAN KABOOMI'S MUM SAY TO HIM WHEN HE WAS NAUGHTY?

Obi-have!

WHY DOES OBI-WAN HATE LARD VADER?

He always knew he was a bit of a dark Force.

WHAT DID OBI-WAN SAY TO THE SHEEP?

May the Force be with ewe!

WHAT IS OBI-WAN KABOOMI'S FAVOURITE DATE?

May the Fourth be with you.

WHY WAS OBI-WAN KABOOMI ALWAYS TURNING UP IN PICTURES?

He loves to photobomb!

DID YOU HEAR ABOUT THE CHICKEN WHO BECAME A REBEL PILOT?

He flew an eggs-wing fighter!

CAN YOU PASS THE KETCHUP, KABOOMI?

Of course. May the sauce be with you.

WELCOME TO THE PORK SIDE!

HOW DO THE MYNHOGS VISIT KING MYNHOG?
Through the bat flap!

WHAT'S JABBA'S FAVOURITE MEAL?
The whole hog.

WHAT DO YOU CALL AN EVIL LEADER DIGGING A HOLE?
Darth Spader!

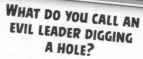

WHERE DOES EMPEROR PIGLATINE TAKE HIS CLOAK TO GET IT CLEAN?
To the dry cloners!

WHAT IS THE MYNHOGS FAVOURITE SPORT?
Aerobatics!

WHAT DID THE MYNHOG MOTHER SAY WHEN HER SON WAS NAUGHTY?
You bat, bat boy!

WHAT DID ONE MYNHOG SAY TO THE OTHER?
Let's hang out together!

WHAT'S JABBA THE HOG'S MIDDLE NAME?
The.

WHY DID THE PIGTROOPERS RUN OFF TO THE CHICKEN FARM?
They needed to re-coup!

GREEDY GUTS!

IF YOU GIVE JABBA THE HOG THREE SWEETS, THEN TAKE TWO AWAY, HOW MANY WOULD HE HAVE LEFT?

It doesn't matter, you'd better start running!

WHICH PORK SIDE LORD WORKS IN A RESTAURANT?

Darth Waiter!

WHAT'S THE BEST DAY FOR SMUGGLING FAST FOOD?

Fry-day!

HOW DID LARD VADER KNOW WHEN YODA BIRD WAS MAKING A CHEESE SANDWICH?

There was a 'grate' disturbance in the Force!

WHY WAS GREEDORK ALWAYS ASKING PEOPLE FOR COCONUT CHOCOLATE BARS?

He was a Bounty hunter!

WHAT IS EMPEROR PIGLATINE'S FAVOURITE PART OF THE DAY?

Breakfast, lunch and dinner!

WHERE DOES TEREBACCA KEEP HIS BISCUITS?

In a Wookiee jar!

WHY DID LARD VADER BURN HIS TOAST?

He liked it on the dark side.

CHUCK 'HAM' SOLO!

WHY WAS CHUCK SOLO THE BEST ACTOR IN THE BIRD ALLIANCE?

He always hammed it up.

WHAT WAS CHUCK'S BIGGEST ROLE?

Hamlet!

WHAT DID SOLO SAY WHEN HE MET YODA BIRD?

I'm your biggest Ham!

WHY DID HAM FAIL HAIRDRESSING SCHOOL?

He was always stopping people from dyeing!

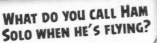

WHAT DO YOU CALL HAM SOLO WHEN HE'S FLYING?
Ham So High!

WHY DID HAM SOLO HIDE WHEN HE HEARD LARD VADER COMING?
He was feeling yellow!

WHY WAS SOLO ON THE RUN?
He was a hamburglar!

WHY DID HAM SOLO VISIT A BANK?
He wanted a bank clone!

WHAT DID HAM DO WHEN HE COULDN'T FIND A DATE TO THE REBELS' BALL?
He went Solo.

MORE YODA!

I THINK YOU SHOULD GO TO THE DOCTOR.

Why?

YOU'RE LOOKING A LITTLE GREEN!

WHAT DO THE PIGTROOPERS WEAR TO A PARTY?
A bow-TIE!

WHAT CAR DOES
YODA BIRD DRIVE?
A toy-Yoda!

WHAT DID YODA BIRD
SAY TO TEREBACCA WHEN HE
DIDN'T HAVE ENOUGH MONEY
TO PAY FOR HIS JUICE?

Do you have two credits?
A little short I am.

HOW DOES YODA GET
THROUGH TRAFFIC?
On his M-Yoda-bike!

WHY DID TEREBACCA BECOME A PILOT?

He wanted to hear some plane speaking.

WHAT DO YOU CALL TEREBACCA WHEN HE WORKS WITH CLAY?

Hairy Potter!

HOW DOES TEREBACCA SOLVE MATHS PROBLEMS?

He works out the hair root.

WHAT'S BIG, HAIRY AND CAN'T STOP EATING BISCUITS?

A Wookiee-monster!

WHY DID TEREBACCA GO OUTSIDE FOR A WALK?

He wanted some fresh hair.

DID YOU HEAR ABOUT THE WOOKIEE WHO MARRIED A SHEEP?

They had a Terebaaaaaaaaacca!

TIME TO GO KA-BOOM-I!

WHY DID YODA BIRD INVITE KABOOMI TO HIS BIRTHDAY PARTY?
He wanted it to go with a bang!

WHAT DO YOU CALL A JEDI IN A GRUMP?
Obi-Wan So Gloomy!

WHAT DO YOU CALL A JEDI WHO LIVES IN THE SEA?
Moby-Wan.

WHY SHOULD YOU NEVER GET INTO AN ARGUMENT WITH OBI-WAN KABOOMI?
Because things are bound to blow up!

WHO'S THE HEAVIEST JEDI IN THE GALAXY?
Obi-tonne.
WHAT DO YOU GET IF YOU CROSS AN ANGRY JEDI WITH A WIZARD?
Obi-Wand Kaboomi!
HELP! THE LIGHTS HAVE GONE OUT!
Use the torch!
WHAT HAS YELLOW AND BLACK STRIPES AND IS GREAT WITH A LIGHTSABER?
O-bee-wan!

COSMIC CACKLES

WHAT DID HAM SOLO SAY TO RED SKYWALKER WHEN HE TRIED TO EAT PASTA WITH A KNIFE?

Use the fork, Red!

WHY DID LARD VADER CROSS THE ROAD?

To get to the Pork Side!

WHAT DO YOU CALL A FIGHT BETWEEN TWO FAMOUS ACTORS?

Star Wars!

WHERE DID JABBA THE HOG GET A TATTOO?

At the Tatooine parlour!

WHY DOESN'T LARD VADER TAKE HIS MASK OFF?
He's got terrible helmet hair!

WHAT'S BLACK, HATES THE BIRDS AND GOES UP AND DOWN?
An ele-Vader!

HOW DOES AN EWOK WALK?
E-walk funny!

WHY IS A DROID MECHANIC NEVER LONELY?
Because he's always making new friends!

ROBOTS FOR DUMMIES

BY ANNE DROID

WHY WAS C-3PYOLK ANGRY?

Because the Pigtroopers knew how to push his buttons!

WHY DID R2-EGG2 GO TO THE MECHANIC?

His circuits were scrambled.

THE A-Z OF DROIDS

BY SI BORG

WHAT IS C-3PYOLK'S FAVOURITE TREE?

The old y'oak tree!

WHAT DOES C-3PYOLK DO IN A FIGHT?

He heads to the eggs-it!

WHERE DOES C-3PYOLK LIKE TO GO ON HOLIDAY?

New Yolk City!

R2-EGG ON YOUR FACE!

WHY IS R2-EGG2 SO CLEVER?

He's a real egg-head!

WHY WAS R2-EGG2 EMBARRASSED?

He was feeling a bit dippy.

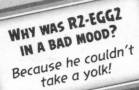

WHY WAS R2-EGG2 IN A BAD MOOD?

Because he couldn't take a yolk!

WHAT DID C-3PYOLK SAY WHEN HE SPOTTED R2-EGG2?

Come in, I've been egg-specting you!

WHY DID R2-EGG2 GO BACK TO DROID SCHOOL?

He thought his skills were getting a little rusty!

WHAT DID C-3PYOLK SAY AT A DROID'S FUNERAL?

Rust in peace.

HOW DID R2-EGG2 BECOME A DROID?

He passed the eggs-amination.

LARD VADER - HE'S LAUGHING ON THE INSIDE!

WHY DID LARD VADER DECIDE NEVER TO GO OUTSIDE?

He wanted to be an in-Vader!

WHY IS LARD VADER SO BAD AT TALENT SHOWS?

He would always choke under the pressure!

WHAT DO YOU CALL A SITH LORD DIPPED IN CONCRETE?

Hard Vader!

WHY DOES LARD VADER WEAR A BLACK CAPE?

His pink one is in the wash.

WHY IS LARD VADER SO ANGRY?

Because he's always seeing Red.

WHEN DID LARD VADER'S JEDI MASTERS FIND OUT HE WAS LEANING TOWARDS THE DARK SIDE?

In the Sith Form.

WHAT IS LARD VADER'S FAVOURITE THING ABOUT WINTER?

Snoooooooooowww!

WHY DOES LARD VADER WANT THE EGG SO MUCH?

He thinks it's eggs-tra special.

WHERE DOES LARD VADER GO TO THE TOILET?

In the Emperor's throne room.

CODE RED!

WHICH DROID LOVES GOING TO THE TOILET?

R2-DPoo!

WHAT IS SMALL, RED AND GOES UP AND DOWN?
Skywalker in a lift.

WHY WAS RED SKYWALKER FEELING A LITTLE BLUE?
Because he was marooned in space.

WHY WAS THE SHEEP FARMER HAPPY TO SEE RED BEFORE HE WENT TO BED?
Red Skywalker at night, shepherd's delight!

WHAT IS A JEDI'S FAVORITE TOY?
A yo-yoda!

WHY SHOULDN'T YOU ASK YODA BIRD FOR MONEY?
Because he's always a little short.

HOW DID YODA BIRD FEEL WHEN RED BROUGHT HOME A NEW LIGHTSABER?
He was green with envy.

WHAT GOES 'TWEET, SWOOSH, TWEET, SWOOSH, OW!'?
Red at lightsaber practice.

DIPPY DROIDS!

WHY SHOULD YOU NEVER WIND UP R2-EGG2?
He's got a short fuse!

WHAT HAPPENED WHEN C-3PYOLK TOLD A JOKE?
R2-EGG2 cracked up!

WHAT DO YOU GET IF YOU CROSS R2-EGG2 WITH A BLOCK OF CHEESE?
An omelette!

WHY DID R2-EGG2 SWAP PLACES WITH A ROBOT FROM MARS?
They were on an eggs-change.

MORE LARDY LARKS!

WHY DOES LARD VADER REFUSE TO FIGHT ON ICE?

Because Red keeps giving him the slip!

WHAT HAPPENS WHEN YOU CROSS LARD VADER WITH THE PIG STAR?

Nobody knows. It's a bit of a grey area!

HOW DID LARD VADER KNOW WHEN TEREBACCA WAS GETTING A HAIRCUT?

He felt a trimmer in the Force!

WHAT DID LARD VADER SAY IN THE SHALLOW END OF THE POOL?

I've been wading for you ...

MOVIE MADNESS!

EPISODE I: THE HAM-TOM MENACE

EPISODE II: ATTACK OF THE SWINE

EPISODE III:
REVENGE OF
SHELL

EPISODE IV:
A NEW HOG

LARD VADER VS RED SKYWALKER!

WHY WAS RED SKYWALKER HAPPY IN THE MAGNET FACTORY?

He could feel the Force!

WHAT DO YOU SAY WHEN RETURNING A RED SKYWALKER FIGURINE TO A SHOP?

Return of the Jedi, thank you.

WHY DID RED EAT PEAS ON THE MIGHTY FALCON?

He thought he might need an escape pod!

WHAT DO YOU CALL PEOPLE WHO ARE WATCHING RED IN BATTLE?

Red Sky-Gawkers!

WHAT GOES
"HA, HA, HA, HA ...
AGGHH ... THUMP!"?
A Pigtrooper laughing
at Lard Vader.

KNOCK, KNOCK.
Who's there?
DARTH VADER.
Darth Vader who?
DAR TH VA DER
COOKIE CRUMBLES!

WHAT DID RED SKYWALKER
SAY TO LARD VADER WHEN
HE SIPPED A FIZZY DRINK?
Pop!

WHY DID LARD VADER
GO TO THE DENTIST?
So he could search
his fillings.

WHAT'S IN A NAME?

WHAT DO YOU GET WHEN YOU CROSS OBI-WAN WITH AN ITALIAN COOK?

Obi-wan Cannoli!

WHAT DO YOU GET WHEN YOU CROSS A BOUNTY HUNTER WITH SOME FRUIT?

Mango Fatt!

WHAT DO YOU GET WHEN YOU CROSS BOBA FATT WITH A PERSONAL TRAINER?

Boba Fit!

WHAT DO YOU GET WHEN YOU CROSS STELLA WITH AN ANGRY TEACHER?

Princess Yeller!

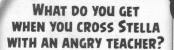

WHAT DO YOU GET WHEN YOU CROSS A MYNHOG WITH A WITCH?

A Mynhag!

WHAT DO YOU GET WHEN YOU CROSS LARD VADER WITH AN ELEPHANT?

An ele-Vader!

WHAT DO YOU GET WHEN YOU CROSS AN EVIL LEADER WITH A PLATE OF CHIPS?

Darth Tater.

THE PORK FEDERATION

WHY SHOULD YOU NEVER TRUST EMPEROR PIGLATINE?

Because he likes to squeal!

HOW DID THE PIG COMMANDER FEEL WHEN THE BIRD ALLIANCE ESCAPED?

Disgruntled!

HOW DID BOBA FATT FEEL WHEN HE GOT A NEW JET PACK?

Uplifted!

WHAT HAPPENS WHEN THE PIGTROOPERS GET HURT IN BATTLE?

They get taken away in a hambulance!

WHAT IS BOBA FATT'S FAVOURITE HOBBY?

Bird spotting!

HAM'S HONKERS!

WHAT DID HAM SOLO SAY WHEN THE EMPEROR SHOT MISSILES AT HIM?

What a blast!

WHY DID HAM HAVE TO SAY EVERYTHING TWICE TO PRINCESS STELLA?

He was on Echo Base.

WHY DID PRINCESS STELLA BUY SPOT CREAM?

Because she was a prisoner aboard the Pig Star but then she broke out!

SAY WHAT?
I MADE YOU SOME TOAST.
It's a bit on the dark side.
What's for dinner?
WOOKIEE STEAK.
It's a little Chewie, isn't it?

WHY COULDN'T THE X-WING PILOT COME OUT TO PLAY?

He was grounded!

WHY DID THE X-WING PILOT LAND IN A TREE?

He was thinking of branching out!

WHERE DID LARD VADER KEEP HIS SPARE CLOAK?

On the Pig Star's main hanger.

WHY DO THE BIRD REBELS PLAY FAIR?

Because anything else would be tweeting!

WHY IS THE MIGHTY FALCON SO SLOW?
Because it takes a millennium to go anywhere.
WHY DID THE BIRD REBEL TAKE HIS SHIP TO THE AUDITION?
He thought it would give him the X factor!
WHY SHOULD YOU NEVER TELL JOKES ON THE FALCON?
The ship might crack up.
HOW DID THE X-WING PILOT FEEL WHEN HE FIRST FLEW INTO SPACE?
Starry eyed!

STARRY SIZZLERS!

WHY DID OBI-WAN FAIL HIS DRIVING TEST?

He refused to turn onto the dark side of the road!

TWO CLONES WALK INTO A SHOP AND THEY BOTH SAY,

"I've seen you somewhere before!"

WHICH BOUNTY HUNTER HAS MONEY PROBLEMS?

Boba Debt!

WHAT DID THE COFFEE SHOP OWNER SAY TO RED SKYWALKER?

May the froth be with you!

EPISODE V
THE EGG-PIRE
STRIKES QUACK!

COSMIC MISH-MASH!

HOW DID THE EWOK CROSS THE ROAD?
E-walked.

WHAT HAPPENED WHEN THE BIRD ALLIANCE FOUND THE PIG STAR?
They penned it in!

WHAT DID YODA SAY TO THE LIBRARIAN?
Due ... or due not?

DOES HAM LIKE TO HAVE ANY HELP WHEN HE'S SMUGGLING?
Nope, he prefers to work solo!

WHY DID RED NOT CROSS THE ROAD?
He got a ticket for skywalking!
WHY DIDN'T YODA GET INTO UNIVERSITY?
Failed the English test, he did.
WHAT'S TEREBACCA'S FAVOURITE HOBBY?
Collecting fleas.
WHAT DO YOU CALL AN EVIL LORD AT A DISCO?
Darth Raver!

JABBA'S JOKES
(LAUGH OR HE'LL SQUASH YOU!)

WHAT DID LARD VADER SAY TO RED SKYWALKER AFTER HE ATE SOME BEANS?

I am your farter.

DID YOU HEAR THAT JABBA THE HOG IS ON A SEAFOOD DIET?

He sees food, he eats it!

WHAT IS LARD VADER'S FAVOURITE FILM?

Men in Black!

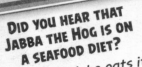

WHAT ARE YODA'S FAVOURITE BISCUITS?

Shortbread.

GAME OVER!

WHAT'S THE TEMPERATURE ON TATOOINE?

Luke warm.

WHAT DO YOU CALL FIVE SITHS ON A LIGHTSABER?

A Sith-kebab!

THERE'S BEEN AN ERROR. THERE SHOULD HAVE BEEN AN ORDER FOR CHOCOLATE ICE CREAM CONES, NOT VANILLA.

Then let the Cone Wars begin!

JOKE MISSION: COMPLETE!

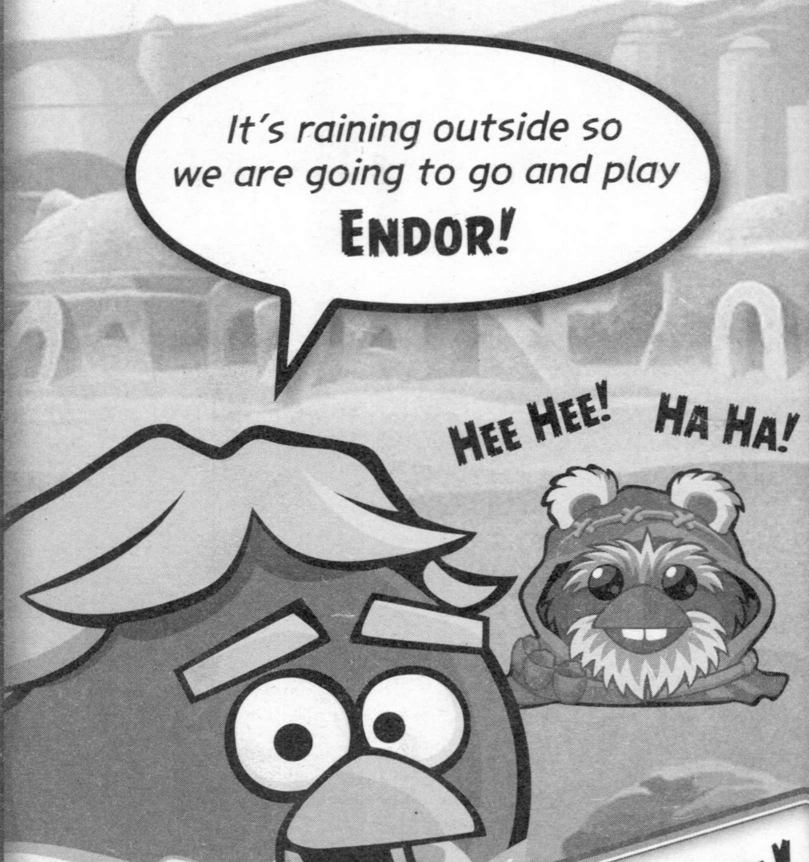